Rules at Home

Sharon Coan, M.S.Ed.

We have **rules** at home.

Rules help us get along.

Be fair.

Be nice.

CHORES DONE
Clean room
Vacuum/dust
Recycling
Take out trash
Put away toys

Be helpful.

Be safe.

Have good **manners**.

Rules help us get along.

Write It!

1. Meet with your family.
2. Talk about your rules.

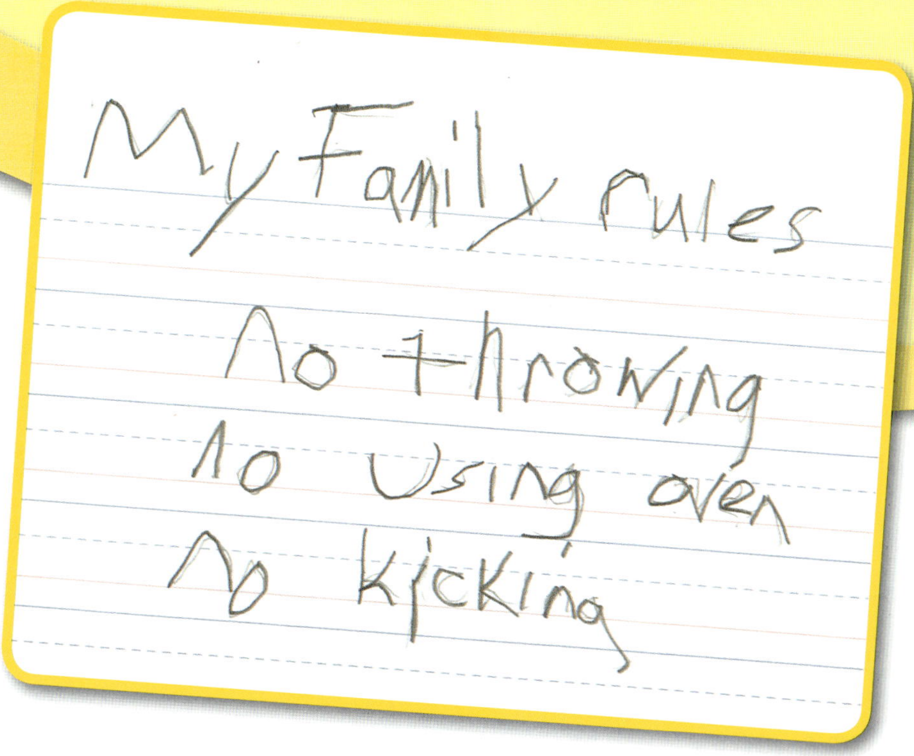

3. Write your family's rules.

Glossary

manners—ways to behave politely

rules—things that tell you what you may or may not do

Index

Your Turn!

Think of a new rule for your family. Tell them about it.

Consultants

Shelley Scudder
Gifted Teacher
Broward County Schools

Caryn Williams, M.S.Ed.
Madison County Schools
Huntsville, AL

Publishing Credits

Conni Medina, M.A.Ed., *Managing Editor*
Lee Aucoin, *Creative Director*
Torrey Maloof, *Editor*
Lexa Hoang, *Designer*
Stephanie Reid, *Photo Editor*
Rachelle Cracchiolo, M.S.Ed., *Publisher*

Image Credits: Cover, p.1, 10 Blend Images/Alamy; p.3 Greatstock Photographic Library/Alamy; p.4 Image Source Plus/Alamy; p.14 RubberBall/Alamy; p.12 Adam Gault/Getty Images; p.17 Jutta Klee/Getty Images; p.8 bo1982/iStockphoto; p.22 ChristopherBernard/iStockphoto; p.24 dejanristovski/iStockphoto; p.13 Mari/iStockphoto; p.9 meshaphoto/iStockphoto; p.7 ozgurdonmaz/iStockphoto; p.11 Yarinca/iStockphoto; Backcover, Diana Kenney; p.19 Teacher Created Materials; All other images from Shutterstock.

Teacher Created Materials
5301 Oceanus Drive
Huntington Beach, CA 92649-1030
http://www.tcmpub.com

ISBN 978-1-4333-7342-8

© 2014 Teacher Created Materials, Inc.
Printed in China
Nordica.012019.CA21801586